FRESH HORSES

Dear Jane
Knowing you
has been so important
to me — you are
a great partner &
a wonderful friend
Mary

FRESH HORSES

POETRY BY GARY LEMONS

VAN WEST & COMPANY · SEATTLE

Copyright © 2001 by Gary Lemons
All rights reserved.
Manufactured in the United States of America.
Printed on acid-free paper.

Library of Congress Control Number: 2001094331
ISBN: 0-9677021-2-7

9 8 7 6 5 4 3 2 1

COVER ART: Susan Rothenberg, "May #2," 1979. Copyright © 2001 by Susan Rothenberg / Artists Rights Society (ARS), New York. Special thanks to Stephanie Lutgring for her assistance in reproducing the art.

AUTHOR PHOTOGRAPH: Nöle Giulini

Van West & Company, Publishers
5341 Ballard Avenue NW
Seattle, Washington 98107
www.vanwestco.com

This book is dedicated to
NÖLE GIULINI
the beautiful seal who lives in the waves of my heart.
Forever is not long enough to love you.

...and not one of these things nor one of these persons is ever quite to be duplicated, nor replaced, nor has it ever quite had precedent: but each is a new and incommunicably tender life, wounded in every breath, and almost as hardly killed as easily wounded: sustaining, for a while, without defense, the enormous assaults of the universe....

—James Agee, *Let Us Now Praise Famous Men*

Contents

1

- 7 Trespassing
- 9 He Runs In Darkness
- 12 Fresh Horses
- 14 Epitaph
- 15 Rivers Running Backwards
- 20 The Girl with Tender Paws

2

- 25 The Understanding
- 26 The Land Outside the Heart
- 33 The Opening of the Always Closed
- 35 Andromeda
- 37 Black Hills
- 38 Borders
- 40 Chanku Wakan—the Sacred Road

3

- 47 Land Mines
- 48 Homeland
- 50 Veterans Day
- 52 Arisen
- 57 LaPush
- 58 Escaping

4

65 The Absence of Miracles
67 Bottle from a Lost Island
72 Freedom

75 *Notes*
79 *Acknowledgments*
81 *About the Author*

FRESH HORSES

It will be difficult
But unfold the victims in yourself
And put them out to sea
With all their sails afire.

Then feel the running strength
Of the horse
Whose riders all have fallen.

I

Trespassing

Every new trail is a script of motion
Frozen into the quiet place where movement
Stops and original grace begins.

The glint of light from the lake
At the end of the path sparkles
Through the trees, unexpectedly
Bright with filtered sun—the dark
Path we have known is gone.

And in its place a beckoning—
We walk on cold stones to the pier
Collapsing into the lake yellowed
By the slow release of blowdown cedar,

Trespass through slender maples
With leaves the size of bear paws
To the edge of water, to the edge of country,

And enter without passport
This cold planet of otter and reflected sky.

We are somewhere near our first selves,
Surrounded by the efforts of our life
To arrive beside a yellow lake
Circled by thorns whose bright berries
Taste of insight and old struggles.

We come shivering from the water
And dry beside a fallen homestead

Imagining the settlers with cattle and children
Whose beliefs were blown to the edge of tolerance…
Now the old beams and rotted ghosts
Tolerate everything the sky can bring them.

You and I have loved before, have built
Our nests in trees and seen them logged,
Have come to each other as if dipping
Into reflections in a lake and now we
May honestly say we are not trespassing

In the tender and eternal somewhere.
We are swimming home in our bodies
To each other—we have taken off our clothes
For the last time in the presence of a stranger.

He Runs In Darkness

They were a very small band of indians
And yes they were off the reservation
But my god it was winter on the Powder—
Where could they go and what could they harm.

In the government shacks the wind
Blew out the candles and the kerosene.
The people were dying from an army
So small it got inside them—

This band chose to own their way of dying in winter,
The hard line of fresh snow on stretched
Hide, the lodge-fire, the warmth of family
Touching under skins, the old ones
Singing on the backtrail in silent country.

But they were off the reservation and soldiers
Caparisoned from the nearest fort and went for them,
Dragging small cannons, wagons, and cold men
With angry hearts along a frozen trail.

The urge for meat was on the tribe;
Twelve children, three women, and ten men
In a running fight against soldiers through heavy winter—

Hunger circles every frozen camp, but
Two hungers circle a running camp—
Ribs like hatchets on the women
Who would not eat the venison

Dried beside a summer fire but softened
It inside their mouths to feed the babies.

It got harder past the snow line, harder to nock
The arrow with the fingers numb, harder
To cover the tracks of dragging litters.

The sun had not risen
When He Runs In Darkness rose from his blanket
And watched the breakfast fires, closer than before,
From the soldiers' camp. Another day, he thought,
Then took his bow into the trees.

A sound inside the forest held him.
He warmed his hands slowly together, then
Placed an arrow, hungry in the early mist.

There on the fallen needles a doe calving,
Eyes rolling, pushing at the bloody head that would not pass.
He Runs In Darkness stroked the deer and spoke its name
Then pulled until the fawn came out, breathed once and died.

The doe was hard and swollen, crusted with ice,
Still pushing, until the second head came out and, easier,
The twin was born, dead before it touched the ground.

The doe was no better for the birthing.
He Runs In Darkness drew his knife,
Speaking softly to the mother of the deer.

And the thing happened—the choosing of
He Runs In Darkness—the doe pushed

Out another fawn, kicking and alive,
That wobbled to its feet, breathed.

When the soldiers arrived they found
The lodges empty, the fires still burning,
And the red prints of the tiny deer
Leading into a dwindling storm.

Fresh Horses

1

You saddle
The beautiful and ride
To the far corners,
Where the fences are cut,
To the beginning of an opening.

Even when our journey
Seems only to be wandering,
We go on,
To the dark stables
Where fresh horses are
Building perfect riders.

2

There are those who think that art
Is something puzzled from extravagance
Left hanging in unnecessary air:

Remember:
There is only the sky,
The ground, and the equipoise of every rider.

The importance of saying the unsaid,
Of creating the unseen, is a way
To thank yourself for being born.

Get back on fresh horses—breathe
Deeply their passion for the effort—
Keep riding, your beings braided
Skin to motion, distance to dream,
In the urgency of going home.

Feel your legs around the breath
Of something living for its journey.
The art is in the getting tired
And changing horses.

3

The winded horse leans against the
Fading light as if the colors of a dying sun
Could hold him up.

No one had thought to wipe him down,
And feed him.

We must deliver ourselves from the past
As we deliver ourselves from each moment,
Even though we share, as riders,
All the exertions of the dismount.

The truth is in the effort; the work
Alone reflects the courage of its author.
The art is in the getting tired
And changing horses.

Epitaph

Done, after unending thought, with life,
I walk to the edge of everything I fear.

Snow forks through layers of warm air
To become the rain that reaches us, falling
As we do, through and toward a distant impact.

Birds mingle with raindrops but never sing
When they are wet. They know the fields
Of silence woven by their flight erupt
In songs behind them, wildfires
Of songs burning up the grass with music—

They teach their young to fly, but not to sing.
This is only learned by living.

Rivers Running Backwards

for the guardian, Chief Joseph

They stood outside the circle near a white tent
Staked in the camas fields your ancestors worked
And refused the pipe of peace as they spoke
In the iron tongue of all conquerors:

"Hear me and listen well. You must gather
Your children, turn in your weapons, and come
To this land provided for you many marches
Away by the Great White Father.
It is a place hospitable to the hoe and seed
And if you are industrious your work
Will bear fruit into the next generation
And your children and theirs will prosper.
This is your only choice, your only offer."

The flag of truce snapped in the high air of Nespelem.
Cavalry and foot soldiers lined up beside the speaker
Whom none among you could believe had spoken these things.
The sweet smells of kouse lifted from fires
Where the winter food was being carefully set aside,
For each season makes a promise of a prayer.

The creaking of the soldiers' saddles
As they shifted rifles over pommels
Was mimicked in the willows by crows.

You are the guardian of your people. When one voice
Speaks for the welfare of all, it is yours:

"What is this place you would have us go where our brothers
Have gone to shake themselves apart
And leave only their ghosts to blow away?
I have seen this place behind my eyes and there are no trees,
No mountains, no animals, only sickness and wind.
What are these tools you would put in my hand
That do not fit my grip nor stir a single tear of joy?
By whose power do you take away our sky,
The shape and shadow of our stories?

"This is where the bones of our old ones lie—
The home of our first ones, the place where
Spirits wander singing to our children.
We will not want to fight, for as long
As memory our people have been friends
To wasicu, but if you come to move us
A little bit of all of us will die—here we stand."

And then the great wheel of death and havoc
Did spin anew—squeaking on its bloody hub,
Rolling out of the seasons onto the lodges
And ponies and babies, milling flesh into gristle underground.

To the north, Canada, freedom, Tatanka Iyotanka
Waiting with hands open, a hard one thousand miles away.
What choice but the sustenance of retreat,
The cold gathering threads of followed flesh?

The dreamers saw the imaginary line shift
Around you, described it as lightning
Trapped inside a violent cloud, as you once saw
A rain of babies in the air…

The line blurred, came close, turned blue,
Grew loud, as from the four directions
The fixed knives charged, firing low
Into the tepees to make sure no small ones lived.

Your people were heroes.
Men and women, raw with sleep, their
Young in their arms, ran through the cordon of battle
Singing their death songs,
Were bayoneted, shot, and ran on

To place the children safely under trees and stones,
Then stumbled through the smoky gauntlet back
To where others stood firing.

Your wife leaned in the pitched door
Of your burning home with three bullets
In her chest and handed you a rifle as she died.

Slowly, under a withering cannonade,
You escaped, the dead on both sides lying strewn
Across the prairie in each other's seeping clothes.

What madness drove the soldiers
That they would slaughter a sleeping village
Under a flag of truce at daybreak?

What deep well of courage, of love,
Preserved your people through
The cold and ambushed miles?

In the end it was the decision to rest
The wounded and the old for one day,

Forty miles from Canada, that allowed
An incompetent pursuit to arrive.

One day of peace, of living the old ways
As if they were not as fragile as frozen
Breath, the good smells from cooking fires,
The people fed and warm...

They found you and paid dearly
That day—everyone did who lived or died.
Another shameful page turned
Over one hundred years ago,
Bookmarked and left unread today.

But there are those of us who learned, Joseph,
Those who unfold your memory
Each time the world becomes, as it is today,
A place where loyalty and courage
And, yes, love beyond the love of self
Lie buried in an unmarked grave.

What was suffered remains forgotten
While what was learned must always
Be dug from the soil by human hands
And resurrected to the shouts of angels
Aiming broken arrows
At the receding face of God.

After every battle, when all the injured flesh
Is stilled and the groaning on the ground
Has ceased, there is at last a momentary peace,
A time for all who lived, who endure to this day,
To watch one another gather up the wounded and the dead...

This is the time for changing skins,
For going back with soldiers from the other side
To see their empty hearts and drink
Directly from the eye their children's tears.

Only then will our stories glow
With a light that makes tomorrow
More than just disputed sunrise.

The Girl with Tender Paws

for Nöle

I

I go where you look—
There I know the flame
Is bluest with the touch of fire.
I live in the body we have made
Under starlight into each other.

Love prefers to ride bareback
Astride dark-eyed horses
Who dream the world in front of them.

I have set in the distance
And watched your spirit
Burning what you feed it in the night,
Have come down from
Remote perceptions and licked
The trees and ground on the dark perimeter,
Slept in the heart of every animal
Whose days surround you,
And waited for anyone I am
To step forward toward this light.

I believe in one thing—
That every day
Our breath becomes tomorrow's wind.

I know the stones have a deep skin
Stretched around a fragile heart,

That love comes into being
When what we believe
Enough to die for
Lets us live.

2

I have never seen, nor shared
The earth in all my days and nights
With anyone like you.
What you touch with your eyes
Is guided toward its hidden beauty,
What you touch with your mind
Becomes brave enough to speak.

3

If I nip the ear of this poem
It is only to excite meaning
From something sensual,
Not linguistic.

If this poem nips my ear,
Or yours,
It is because you, too,
Should be loved
By someone like yourself.

So I believe in you
And place one hand on my heart,
The other on my work…

I go where you look,
Knowing you are fierce,
Beautiful, and true,
And that I love you.

2

The Understanding

We are forests cut by streams,
Roads to carry water to the sky.

We are rivers threading forests
And our faces stepping-stones.

We are the first and last light
Of a billion-year-old fire
Visible to every eye but ours.

We are the entire natural world
And we are in pieces.

We are everything that survives death
And everything ever buried in the ground.

We are the love in each other's heart
And we are the bullet in the barrel.

We are the hurricane created
By the wings of one forgiving bird.

The Land Outside the Heart

1

Forever is to everything the same star fading…

2

A creature crouches in blackberry
Thorns nursing slashed hands, its feet
Sunk deep in wet ground, its conscience
Formed in retreat, sustained in exile
By memories of love eaten to survive—
Somewhere dogs upon its trail

Sniff footprints filled with blood
And hunger for a brighter moon—
The creature hears them, untangles
From its heart yarns of memory
And threads forgiveness into moonlight,
Is swallowed from the sight
Of anything not sure it lives today.

Blood down—its fingers,
Inverted, become the canteen…
It drains itself to live—

Now rising from hiding, dancing
With thorns and shadows,
It moves where we move when we,

Into a thicket dripping blood, jettison
Our essence and, unladen, stagger on.

It is ours, this being torn from flesh
And made to shift outside our skin
For affections it creates from solitude.
Ours, too, its beautiful, nocturnal face.

3

Sleeping or still, our breath
Floats in tissue filled
With quiet ponds of blood
Where imaginary horses come to wet
Their velvet muzzles in the moon
That sinks inside our willingness to love.

When one moon falls from view
Another loops across the sky
Darkened by so many final breaths
Our lives appear as revenants in fields
So harvested not even soil remains.

Every animal lives inside another
Until born, rejoicing
On the wind from mother
Into mother since the crawling family,
Ageless through the feminine,
To stand beneath a yellow star
That marks our winnowed bodies
To be scattered where it shines.

Hope is the wind that never slackens,
Love the current when becalmed.

4

When we awaken ourselves
We hold the injured
Creature crying in the thorns—

There is nothing sadder
Than our little faces
Smiling in still water,
Our image caught
In brimming spoons,

No smaller way of dying,
No oblique cruelties
That suffer the little children
To be broken into stones…

Every breath is a weight tossed
Into the red pond of tomorrow, stampeding
The shy horses that stand in blood
And drink the ripples ending
Where our hearts are healing.

5

We have caught the creature slowed
By carrying all it loves with damaged hands
Only to find our own hands bloody.

It is we who await us. Know,
In the bright waves on the lifeboat,
Taking water, signaling with a final flare,
That what we hunt is who we are:

The carrion angels flushed from daylight
When all our inhalations end,
Feeding on the frothing spirit,

The small, staked horses
Hobbled to an endless sky
Inside the house of bones.

6

The land outside the heart
Lies undiscovered; only
The brave risk dying far from home.

We are accompanied by the shifting
Image taking shape ahead
And leave behind foundations
For the cities others settle.

It is enough to sit alone
And love the evening sun
As it falls off the earth
Knowing, even as we shift
Between the colors of a distant light,
We are horizons…

We are rising from ourselves
To live inside the skin
Around a larger star.

7

The moon has only its short time
To play in the fields of smoking suns…

The creature cannot be free in daylight,
For all its frailties can be seen
And who it is roots toward earth
While what it isn't is pursued…

Now is the time, while we sleep,
While the moon spins around the pillow
And the clock in the blood
Sweeps its hands across the heart,
To call them all back home—
All the pieces puzzled by our absence
That together form a life unlived.

Surely it is clear that tomorrow
Comes, no matter where we are,
To the stones, to the sky,
To the whole of all abundance
And emptiness that, rubbed
Together, spark the wildfire
Burning the habitat behind us.

8

The land outside the heart lies
Unclaimed, will always be a sparrow,
Too late to join its kin in flight,
Freezing in the hollow of a snowbound tree.

Meaning we are not winter birds
Limp in the hot branches of summer
But summer birds whose heated spirals
Lie dormant under codes of cold…

To rise from our nests with hot wings
Into the chill of living without love
Under a skeletal moon
To touch once more inside our chests
The starting place of sky,
Is how we know we are horizons,

How we know we thaw from sleep
Into the form of something flying home.

9

We lie still in the deep night
While leaves angle from their stems
And rocks creep on other rocks—
We are open and the universe pours in.

Our hands bleed from the work of life.
They hold our days and nights,
Swing between vines, and toughen.

We are alone in the thorns, dripping
Our scent upon receptive ground,
While hunters tighten imaginary circles.

We are inside and outside ourselves,
Wanting back out and back in, wanting love,
Wanting to see beyond the conclusions of death—
Wanting everything to stop trembling.

The Opening of the Always Closed

The wind blows everywhere today,
Its song in the throats of grasses,
In the voices of small creations,
Everywhere its hand on our face
As we turn into each other.

All the world is the wind's.
Freedom, which we seem to need
But in our lives so seldom find,
Is, to the wind, a gift never opened,
Left behind where it's been.

I speak of the wind on this still day
Because the opening of the always closed
Has occurred in me and in you.

We believe in the goodness of the grave,
Raise totems to the places flesh can never go,
Seldom touching, while we can,
The songs streaming from our hearts
Into and beyond each other's hands.

Now I touch you, and wonder
If compassion makes us sick
Or can it heal a wound that never bleeds?

From our mouths, from our eyes, from
All we are a wind is coming with a gift.
Will we know enough to keep it?

When the sun burns off the night,
And all the smoke of evenings
Spent within the tiny light
Of lives that sleep and beat alone
Dispels into a woven breath,
There will come a stillness to the world
And loving you will be the only wind.

Andromeda

Old friend—we walked three
Terraced meadows into and then
Beyond the bottom of a tangled blueberry seep.

We walked unaware of any presence
In the brooding shrubs hung with
The purple stars of a season's toil;
We were new to forever
And trusted the field was ours.

You said that growing old
Was a good thing for poets—that all our lives
We'd write as if humility is vice
Until the realization every
Word's a drop of blood
Stands up inside our heads and turns
The mirrors toward the wall.

But you died before you could realize
How right and wrong you were—maybe
Dying young makes a young poet older.
Maybe at the end our eyes are open.

At the edge of vision, as we walk, an egret
Balances on one foot, then flashes its beak
And swallows something without regret.

To work for something and achieve it
Is to be given faith in the impossible.
To choose life and be refused it

Leaves a drinking straw inside the heart
Through which miracles are sipped.

But nothing was refused that day, not
The birds who called across the sky
To tell each other where love is,
Not the footsteps filling up with water—

Now that you are gone I spend more time
In the garden, digging in the ancient
Earth from which the dead arise.

Black Hills

Believe in the air of roses here
In a place of fallen stone and bitter pine.

Believe in the water in the canteen
Extracted, mouth-warm, from dry rivers.

Believe that love is a business
Whose overhead is financed by lust
And you will absorb fire and darken
Without warmth in the painted light.

Believe in the dead. They are your parents
And grandparents. They are you.

For one moment of unguarded belief I
Would turn as still as these ancient rocks
And be happy never to move again.

Borders

San José, Costa Rica

I

Mornings begin with horns, the swordplay
Of iron gates, emptied garbage cans,
And the whispers of school children
Walking in uniform between fruit stands
Where bright globes hold the light of yesterday.
The migration of our rarest birds begins here…

Then bells to remind us we are alive,
How we are beautiful as vendors' fruit.

I watch the lame woman
On the hot stones
In the unremitting morning
Spread her injured legs
Into the path of tourists…

The cut necks of the flowers
She sells bleed the fields of sun
That grew them, sweetening
The gummy street into a burning paste…

Somebody dreaming she is shrinking
In a sea of faces streaming past
Like particles of smiling light
Cannot hope to have a fork for every child.

We must know the vilest things
Occur as the poem is written.

2

The Bribri, who live beneath
Greenery so thick the sky is holy,
Have a legend that withstands conquistadores—

It says the earth emits the ghosts
Of those who die protecting others
Into space where they turn to stars
Whose light comes back to us as children…

I believe this: that at every border
Truth masquerades as someone
Leaving as you are walking in.

There are mirrors in the jungle.
You must close your fist around the air
And squeeze it until something is set free.

Chanku Wakan—the Sacred Road

Wounded Knee

1 GHOST DANCE

We come to a place beside a frozen river
Where the blue sparkling ice turns
The quilt of withered grasses
Into starfields the distant sun
Wanders singing of summer conquests:

We come because we need one another to go on.
What we hold dear grows dim in snares behind us:

Here on this frozen river we whittle
From the sky and earth the lyrics of our common song.

It is for you that I give up the old ways
And the comfort of each desperate measure to survive.
It is for me that you have come so far
To stand beneath a spare moon
In a blue field and make a medicine of love.

We will rise up again.
We will learn from
All that enters softly, on quiet feet,
The temples erected both now and forever
In ourselves upon this holy ground…

Only the hills smoking with coyote breath
And night birds falling into day birds

Sleeping on a single bough will
See these ground fires, our bodies dancing.

Power is not a thing acquired by purpose.
Power is a crow on one leg hopping.
Power is not taken from others or given.
Power is wind arranging worlds into worlds.

Power is not violence or strength or even beauty.
Power is a gathering of gentle skins
Around the landing of an ancient light.

In the cold night the sound of the river freezing
Is like horses nickering on open range
Across miles of darkness, to each other.

2 Chankpe Opi Wakpala — the Stream

Where we gather in harmony the soldiers blow
Into brass the anger of the unreprieved.
They are not satisfied with killing the self
That rides them, or the self created by dismounting.

They covet the music of peace to force
Through bugles a sound that stops
The heart of all things living — the owls falling
Into the white feathers of the snow, the wolf
High in the timbers, its cry kindling fire
On its winter coat, the people, their stories
And their visions, pushed through brass
And narrowed into foreign thunder.

Many died here and passed into a place
Where the faces of the ghost dancers
Move in and out of our stories
Like lost bears in a bottomland.

It is to the men and women
Who would take us to our fallen kin
As they rise up from the earth
With our names upon their wounds
That we must turn, in the cold night
When the geese are leaving,
For a reason to regather.
For all of us are killed when one of us is killed.

Yet here, we move near cold water
In a blue and white meadow, pierced,
Strung together and slow to bleed,
That by our fatal deepening
The lives of those to come
Draw light and water
From the land, now, by treaty, left only in the air.

3 Abebeya—The Scattering

When Tatanka Iyotanka was murdered,
Blood dripped from the mouths and noses of the people
As they awoke to dance in the frozen sheets of ice
Outside their lodges. He said, when asked what he thought
Of indians signing away the lands of their heart,
"Indians, there are no more indians—I am the last."

And yet his people, the Hunkpapa, the Mniconjou, the Oglala, the Brule,
The Yanktonais, the Teton, the Sans Arc, the Santee, the Blackfoot Sioux,
Came to dance their dead to life again,
To place their feet upon the bloody
And impossible sod, to learn eternal things
Lie waiting only in eternity, where Christian angels
Occupy an afterlife partitioned by the gun.

We gather not to endure, because that will end,
But to die, knowing that our arms around one another
Is all that's left of God.

3

Land Mines

It has eyes.
It knows the altitude of birth
And the shy ticking of the rain.

It sees the color of the sky
As monochrome waiting
For a streak of red.

It knows the heat of openings,
Of entrance, knows how to fall
And where to land.

It is kin to nothing
That lives beneath it or
Beyond it in the air.

It is ice inside a solar dream,
Warmed by contact, hungry,
Living for a single meal.

It is nothing new to the earth—
It is a thrown thing, a fired thing,
An angry word or withheld touch.

It is waiting in every animal,
For every animal, the bridge
Between two moments over blood.

Homeland

The young field hands are spread
Against the white adobe wall,
Touched by knives to keep them still.

They were cutting cane with wet
Bandannas around their heads when
The soldiers appeared like a shimmering
City at the edge of day, riding
Through the green cane unopposed.

The workers watched them come
But did not run—where would they go?
They dropped their machetes
So it could not be ordered
To shoot them for resisting.

As the soldiers face them toward the wall
One braver than the rest stops praying.

They smell the brown resin of the cane
On their clothes and bodies and hear
The saddles of the soldiers' ponies
Shifting in the heat.

Overhead the unshielded bowl of the sun
Gives off the heated brass smell of a bullet
That has lost its speed and is slowly
Dropping from the air.

What happens next depends on
Whose story you believe and whether
The village priest gets drunk before confession.

What is certain is the workers in the field
Were not allowed to turn around and see
Their village burning behind them—

Maybe now they stand with feet
Spread wide in the soil of their homeland
And witness for eternity the resurrection of hope
In the eyes of descending black birds.

Veterans Day

Between the moment when stars
Rule the cold subservient kingdom
Of closed portals and stitched eyes
And when the sun climbs
The old road and snaps the necks
Of lamps across the quiet city, everything
Alive shares a cradle with the dead.

A soldier stands beside his bed holding
Pictures of young friends now gone,
Atomized in a haze of youthful fire.

The soldier grows old and they do not.
They sit in wooden frames and wait
For time to get the distance right
And lob its final mortar.

We know, in our dreams and prayers,
That all the dead surround us,
That they touch us in ways we're not prepared to feel.
There is comfort in knowing this.

In every war some come home and some do not
And some do both. This man is deciding whether
To save the mouth that uses toothpaste
Or the mouth that spits the cork.

This man has horses tied to his arms
With invisible wire and they are galloping
In opposite directions away from him.

He remembers a few things about today
But everything about yesterday: the dew
Glistening on tripwire, the bad wallpaper
Job inside the conscience, the floral
Code of a foreign sun casting geometric shadows—

He writes in the last page of his diary, "How
Can you eat ghost butter and not spread death?"

What must be said is that once the lamps
Are put out the darkness will no longer
Be his. It will be ours…

This is the experience of soldiers and light,
Of growing older and growing no longer:
There are particles of every moment blowing
From forever through the garden of our days
Where we toil with our hands buried deep
In the flesh of last year's harvest.
Our survival is a miracle that never ends.

Arisen

1

Falling into sleep from the wet edge of life,
Our bodies tire of forever
In a place their spirits will not touch them.

I draw a picture of your face,
Fingering lightly in this darker air,
And pass into the dream of loving you:

Without dialogue water rises and boats
Approach from every side and board us at will;
Occupied, without effort or consent,
In this way the dreamer is bent to the dream.

2

In this other earth are clues to our nature
And in this instrumental earth
We find the place where being is restored,
Much more than a peopled emptiness.

It is the place we stand without posture.
For some, it is a simple, unendurable pain
And all the music they have drained from other throats.
For some, it is soil between flowers,
A place protected by the wind.

3

The path between seeing and knowing
Is traveled by suicides in raw transitions
Toward places of death or dying…
Places found only by those who cannot speak
But live by listening to the soldiers falling,

Each into each, in the clamoring fields,
Falling into the harvest, into the wheat,
And corn and, yes, into the bread,
Dying at the very beginning of believing.

We are all soldiers, children who wear
Our bones outside our skin, who grow
Up and starve all over again.

We are the hatchling angel breathing
In the coffin's vacant air,
Half-alive, half a nonexistent god, sealed
Inside our days by the work of our hands.

4

There is one light upon us all.
A desert sun cooking mirages from the sky
Into a still-life of gouting
Pilgrims, their wagon-boards smeared
With faith and blood, their beasts
Unburdened in a silent land
Under a dreamed sun loving that it burns.

There is this brightness upon us all:
Stone arrows fly into the meat of settlers
Who would come to a place and unsettle it.

Only the dead know the distances
We cross each time we touch.

In our dream, death repeats itself,
Reminding us of its nearness,
Its interest in our well-being.

We are traveling without guidance
Through the lessons of a new terrain: Remember,
Where there is no tenderness, there is invasion.

Asleep, we are invisible to death.

5

I dream you descend a ladder
Into a field planted with women
Who are sisters of your flickered selves.

It is twilight and a moon would like to shine
But you arrange the darkness and keep working—
The stars alone strengthen each of you with light.
The day is over but the work goes on.

In this way the years to come will rise
From sleeping faces touched by angels
Thirsting at a dream where they are captured

By human effort and made to draw
Their water from our well:

They are arisen,
Like us, and must watch
Our final moment tangled
In an edge of purple
And eat it on a thorn.

In this way, the dream is bent to the dreamer.

6

The beginning of wisdom is the end of innocence
As the beginning of death is the end of life.
We come to each other from extremes
Of tenderness and malice with sleep
The country in between.

If we were to love something more than ourselves,
We would rise above our journey with canteens
Filled with angel's blood to toast
The glory of each footstep as it blazes.

7

Each time the dream calls we come,
As a bird flies through an open window
To a child and lets itself be touched,
So we respond when called by love
And remember birdsongs when awakened.

We are all angels, that is the secret we awake to forget.
Let us promise never to be soldiers without wings.

8

In the fog a red bird circles,
Singing of a time when
Sound and color and form
Were not measured in bolts of skin
But in acreages of life outside the body;

The bird knows it is so small,
Is not ashamed to be a dream
Between the earth and air.

I reach the dream of loving you
And retract the bird into sleep
To filter from its song a reason
To rise and remember not just
How to fly but where to land…

The world groans with newborn angels
And soldiers. Love is a dream, yes,
But real once nobody dreams it.

We awaken on the highest branch
And risk our lives each time we choose to sing.

LaPush

We walk to the end of land together,
To the earth's end where water
Blesses then baptizes sky.

You work into the wind, a force
As you move equal to any storm-
Driven bird carried into thunder.

You are the one whose hand is sought
By God when devils moan.

Here the Quileute carved cedar logs
Eroded by waves from forests onto sand,
Carved them with stones by hand,
Then paddled out to touch the sun.

Here the membrane of life was thick enough
To keep each child upheld, thin
Enough for blood to pass into another.

There is a stillness in the fury of waves
That reminds me of you when you are working
With your hands, just before
The being in the shape emerges.

We who have loved, holding nothing back,
Dream of trees turning into vessels
Taking something sacred home.

Escaping

for Roger Lemons
Vietnam, 1968

I

There is an urge to collapse, to let them
Put their finger in your ear, running into the brush

From an escort with translucent hands.
A few trees away the dying are being made dead

By the point instead of the round. Monkeys
Are chattering, ripping orchids apart

And tossing them into your wounds.
Keep moving, the breath a locomotive in the ear,

A driving wheel so loud it scatters dipping birds
Who imitate the rotors that invade their nests.

You have been saved to be the subject of birdsongs.
Exhausted, a tracer in the jungle air.

There is nothing you can do for the ones left
In the thick elephant grass seeing nothing

Of the rain that pours into their open eyes.
You can only, maybe, save yourself.

2

War is a thing that is never over for a soldier.
It slithers in the blood, eating the apples

In the garden of a young man's life, it
Rides in the currents treading water—

It cannot be drowned but reincarnates
Throughout a single lifetime every time it's killed.

3

You have slept beneath the roots of banyan
In a black pool slick with larvae and blood.

It is a fable to be told beside a darkened bed in a nursery
Where tiny animals hang from strings—

Nothing can be picked up where it left off…tropical
Winds ripple the black pool—your blood continues

To drip from a number of holes into the sick water
And out there the runner, whose baton is the lie of complete

Consciousness, is approaching faster.
It is a source of unending wonder how beautiful death can be—

How egrets can rise into a pink sunset from the same
Shimmering water where brand-new ghosts are swimming.

4

You remember a graduation party. Tinkling glass. Not yours
But an older brother's—this is your party—you are coming

Out right now, a debutant crawling through mud
Away from an escort good at backtrailing,

Good at placing the corsage in the middle of the chest.
Their language, somewhere near, sounds like a demon

Dying with human bones stuck in its throat. You
Crawl from the trees into a field of rice and float

Away in one foot of water, escaping without mercy
For your comrades in the valley of the black flag.

God is cruel and subtle. God is underwater with you
Even now, giving you courage while signaling the hunters.

5

Somehow you get through the day and slide
Into the night the way the wailing of slaves

Emanates from everything made of cotton.
Behind you soldiers continue to stab the water

And grasses with long blades with your name on their edges.
If you are alive tomorrow you know you will live forever.

6

Drifting in from sleep or thought we know you
Are safe because a snapshot arrived showing you

Pouring water from a helmet onto your armpits—
We see you and all the solemn processions

Of young men sent to war who came home
To one-man bands and parades on other planets,

All of them called survivors who are expected
To pass the milk again at dinner

And tickle the children and get on with their lives—
We see them marching toward the homeland

And they are shedding memories along the way,
A trail of broken boughs burned by friendly fire;

They are shedding so much we expect them
To have new skins and they do. But they

Are no longer our children though they are
Bloody and innocent as the day they were born.

4

The Absence of Miracles

The world denies itself in me again
While I affirm its best intentions.
From my window I see
The fields around the house steaming
In the early light that rooks anoint.

A sister is walking toward the garden
While singing birds refresh her faith.
She is the one to place the flowers for today,
Whose colors poke into our borderlines.

When we are together
We sing before our simple meal,
"The world is a tiny animal entrusted to our care."

In the fields the sun finds me
Pushing soil into a finer version of itself,
That it may do the same for me.

My sisters move as I do,
Hands around a faceless clock,
Stopping where complexity demands.
In the cool earth the seeds we plant
Are unlike our flesh, stirring
Without wonder toward abundance.

Our lunch is ample; we have none,
But work the ripe fields until dark,

When our eyes see what the earth sees,
Our ears hear what the seed hears.

We do not speak, but sit in heated moment after labor
Beside opening flowers, and make in silence our loud prayers.

Bottle from a Lost Island

I

The voice that is singing to us is different voices.
From storage, we hear ourselves as drying water,
Soundproofed from things.

Ships go down beyond in drying bays:
They glide in high winds toward us
But we repulse them as we become apparent.

For them? They must think of the wandering
Of land, and the inevitable appearance
Of our gestures in their telescope.

They think we want passage. We endanger their water,
My solitaire. They remain offshore,
Nightly stealing the flotsam of our inattention.

What bed is without singing? All the water cannot
Cover is loved by the air, and as perches, we are birds
Upon birds. This is our sleep, the tossings,

Rigs, balsam, all gone down and come up elsewhere,
Bottles in the wireless sea which strangers come upon,
And are startled

By the beggarly worded request for assistance.
Mildewed by the departure of friends, we tower
To full height and blot out the sun.

2

This nightmare the sailor has of shipwrecks,
This fear of being alone, of facing his own address,
Will teach him to float and ram sharks.

We could say the water has been stolen, or completely
Used, but how would the explanation be offered? Is
It enough to shake the hand of the world, without wearing gloves?

Can we dismiss the song, and the sailor,
As obvious, see ourselves artless as spray,

And start again with the voice, steeping
In bawdy unremembering the infusions of tomorrow?

There is a moment when we know
We are literature, and we become aware of only the language
Of our instance, the disjointed prose of our lives.

From this moment we become wicked and open pawnshops
For the imagination. We defend Oscar Wilde with his own
Words, when we say self-contempt is an artist

Whose works decorate the frequented parlors of our age.
We roll up seaweed on the rocks,
And drive the exhausted swimmers from our beach.

The sight of their failing stroke is exciting.
I think the drowned are the best of the dead.

3 Sonnet

Auden, growing old, unpublished "In Memory of W. B. Yeats."
He read too many magazines about the state
Of the country, and told Berryman not to write.
He wrote about murdering a future wife.
And now we must forgive him every stupid thing he said,
For moral passage, for living on, totally bled
By the littering winds that creased and flung his pages
Into the critical eye of a cretinous age.

Unlike Auden, we do not hear of crowds
At Oxford, come to hear Eliot. I could tell you
There will be dangerous refueling maneuvers in midair,
Impossible repairs,
And new extinctions in the human zoo;
We will bring the swimmers ashore to be toweled
And then return them to deep water
Where they will drift toward a farther merger.

4

An old man is dancing with his older wife
In a room where they were introduced. There is
No music but unremembering, and the
Sadness of the deer in the wallpaper.
The man has stumbled and is being led out
By the woman. *Remember, it is not the deer,*
But the wallpaper in which the deer appear.

Grandchildren play in the garden, pretending
To be decorous: the couple, having slept together
In hammocks, are now walking beyond the garden,
On a deer run, imitating different birds

And looking away when the sun illumines
Their faces, falling through the branches.
Without hurting them, I attempt to intrude,
Telling them one of the children
Has fallen into the pond, but they are traveling,
They are traveling now, maybe exhausted and swimming.

5

All of our heroics, piled beside the stars,
Appear tiny; still, they are ours.

6

What we are left with is a child in a pond.
His brother is fishing him out with a stick, but
We must go on describing this, that something
Astonishing might appear. We do not see

The shipwrecks, those grave cows, or the
Old couple, or the swimmers, boats, or
The water evaporating too slowly. (This may
Still be felt as dampness leaving the collar.)

Like pastured cattle, our memory presents us
With the difficulties of recognition; we see

Ourselves spread across infinite acreage,
And the act of remembering is much like feeding time,
When all the cattle converge beside
A gate in low darkness, where, for a moment,
They are one thing in the eyes of one another.
Then, they go to the farther, most broken, fence.

And the sun is not orbiting, but receding.
Having dressed, we are no longer
Interesting through the keyhole.

7

I am losing friends. I am asking them to leave.
Every winter must be wintered.
Every thought startles blackbirds
From the broken masonry around the pond.

The snow falling upon the house, the
Nothingness of snowbound pages, the tracks
Of different-size animals, and the disturbing
Sight of my own footsteps, is everywhere, behind me.

It is deadly, walking the new snow.
I return from the pond with the hide
Of an otter I will spend the winter reviving.
If I cannot restore its life,
Its corpse shall be placed on the pile of my failures
Downstream, that it will not be remembered in this world.

Freedom

1

From the common yard we share with others
Too injured, too cold in their eyes, too
Fearful or tenured to leave, you can see
The woman with the small dog on the hill.

She loves you. She is the life you would live
Were you not enclosed behind your wounds.
She grows smaller, the music of her voice
More quiet, every day of your diminishment.

2

Each day is a room forgetting makes into a prison.
Inside there are iron bars, cruel guards,
Wardens and dogs, our blood on the perimeter.
Outside there is our life.

We have no weapon, no key, no sorcerer's
Wand to make a door, only the image
Burned into each newborn child of freedom.

We must never forget that we are intended
To walk in sunlight, that injury is not a blessing,
That outside there is someone who loves us,
Who may be drying up from lack of rain,
Who needs us to blow down the house
We built with every blow we've taken.

3

Someone waits for all of us beyond our cell.
Perhaps there is a small spotted dog, growing
Older seven days to our one, a child
Or children trying on a larger shoe…
We must never stop working to be free.

You can escape if you remember
A time you were not a guest in your own house.
Then you see them on the distant
Hill, waving you closer, calling your name—
They are the ones who draw a circle on the ground.
At the edge of every darkness love is burning candles.

If you are not at home in yourself then you are dying.
You are lost inside the prison of your days
While tomorrow turns to ashes at the edge.

You must remember now. You must look
Clearly at what it is you hope to never see
About yourself and suffer visions summoned
From the terrors you have turned to brutal light.

You must take off your clothes and place
Them on the shadow growing smaller
Where you stood when you were still afraid.

Notes

TRESPASSING
There is a wonderful thing that occurs in high mountain lakes that are mostly untouched by human activity. The lakes become colored by the predominant leaves and woody debris that fall into them: fir makes for green water, alder tints toward red, and cedar, because of the heavy oil in the wood, turns the lakes a distinct yellow; the natural windfall, over the years, acts much like tea leaves and steeps a very beautiful color and taste in the cup of the lake.

HE RUNS IN DARKNESS
(Please note that in keeping with contemporary agreement among the less conservative leadership of indigenous people in North America, the word "indian" is not capitalized.) This poem is a constructed legend based on the experiences common to many of the tribes who were deposed from their homelands on the plains during the last quarter of the nineteenth century. The Powder (Maka Blu Wakpa) is a river in Montana and Wyoming that was the traditional hunting and wintering grounds for the Shoshone, the Cheyenne, the Crow, and the Lakota. Crazy Horse (Tasunke Witko) became a ghost here and Red Cloud (Mahpiya Luta) held out against the first wave of invaders here. It was and is holy ground. A *running camp* is an old cavalry expression that means to never unpack or unsaddle—essentially it means to be ready to move, which generally describes most indian camps after the white settlers appeared.

RIVERS RUNNING BACKWARDS
This poem is dedicated to the Nez Perce Chief Joseph. It is a historical composite of several of the battles fought during the exodus from Idaho to Canada, and draws most notably from the battle of White Bird Canyon, the battle of Big Hole, and the final encounter, the battle of the Bear Paws. The Nez Perce, against the advice of Joseph and other War Chiefs, rested

the people for one day forty miles from the Canadian border and freedom. It was this last rest that allowed General Miles and his soldiers to catch them. The Nez Perce intended to join Sitting Bull (Tatanka Iyotanka) and his small band of Sioux living in the Grandmother's Land (Canada). The history of this courageous and masterfully strategic flight is well-documented. The words attributed to indian and white speakers are accurate summaries and not the actual quotes. Chief Joseph was an articulate and lyrical orator. It was his statement to General Howard—the Nez Perce would remain in their homeland until "the rivers run backwards"—that became the title for this poem. (Nez Perce is spelled without the accent over the final "e" according to tribal preference.)

Kouse is a root found on the Camas Prairie, traditionally dug by the Nez Perce for its nutritional value to this day.

CHANKU WAKAN—THE SACRED ROAD

This poem is about the massacre that occurred at the small stream, Chankpe Opi Wakpala, or Wounded Knee. The Sioux, under the leadership of the Hunkpapa Chief Bigfoot, gathered at this stream, in the coldest part of winter, to practice their religion, the Ghost Dance, in peace—to initiate their tribe in sacred ritual on holy ground for the purpose of uniting the tribe in a time of trouble. The U.S. Cavalry attacked and killed them there. The bodies of the dead remained frozen in the snow where they fell until the next spring when relatives were allowed off the reservation to retrieve and bury the remains. The importance of the land as a holy gathering place, as a "church" has never been understood by white culture. Instead it has been seen as threatening, and when indians have gathered in one place to heal themselves through the practice of their beliefs they have often been regarded with suspicion—many times they have been dispersed, often with violence. Tatanka Iyotanka is the Lakota name for Sitting Bull. This poem honors the love of tradition and tribal identity that has endured to this day in indian culture.

Escaping

This poem is for my brother Roger Lemons who, as a seventeen-year-old Marine, fought during the North Vietnamese Tet Offensive in 1968. Putting a finger in an ear is an act of disrespect and humiliation used by drill sergeants on new recruits, one of the milder methods of breaking down and diminishing an individual so he can be reconstructed as a soldier. The line "God is cruel and subtle" is a refutation of Einstein's pronouncement to Niels Bohr that "God is subtle but not cruel."

Bottle from a Lost Island

Porpoises and some dolphins defend themselves from sharks by ramming them in the gills. If the gills are damaged severely enough, the shark suffocates. Oscar Wilde, if he did not actually say those words in part 2, certainly could have. Auden in his elder years tried to recall all the copies of his collected works that included the poem "In Memory of W. B. Yeats," for reasons that are unfathomable to me and purely his own. Auden also told a young John Berryman that he could more usefully employ his time as a butcher or a traffic cop than as a poet. Berryman told me this story with a smile on his face.

Acknowledgments

A list of the many family members, friends, and strangers who have helped this pilgrim along the way would be more extensive than this book can allow. I would like to thank the following people for their contributions to my life and, consequently, to my art. Without them, their love, teachings, inspiration, and essential goodness, my life may have strayed to a place where these poems would not have found me. I would be much less than whoever I am without them. My love and gratitude to:

Gregory Jerozal *Sam Hamill*
Bill O'Daly *Kay Lemons*
Rudi Schuster *Dorothy Nestor*
Pam Kolacy *Norman Dubie*
Angela Farmer *Ruth Haycraft*
Victor Van Kooten *Lucinda Williams*
Erich Schiffmann *Danny Little Bear*
Sharon Doubiago *Daryl Dakota*
Jannecke Zevenbergen *Charlie Nestor*
Alison Roth *Charles Haycraft*
Maggie Butler *Bill Glass*
Roger Lemons

My wonderful parents, Jim Lemons, Martha Lemons, Helen Whittall, and Larry Whittall

Mary Jane Knecht for her esteemed friendship, her sweet precision, and her belief in my work

I am very grateful to publisher Jenny Van West for her editorial assistance throughout the evolution of this book. Her love of poetry, her courage, and her wisdom account for much of what may glisten here.

About the Author

GARY LEMONS has been an ironworker, carpenter, tree planter, logger, crane operator, fruit picker, documentary videographer, and arts educator. His poems have been published widely in literary journals, including *Paris Review*, *Iowa Review*, *Kayak*, and *Willow Springs*, anthologized in *Dalmo'ma*, and recorded on the CD *Arisen*. He lives in Port Townsend, Washington, where he manages PTTV, the community television station.

BOOK DESIGN and composition by Jennifer Van West. The typeface is Galliard, designed by Matthew Carter in 1978.